PASCALE HEDELIN - LOU RIHN

SUPERSIZE CROSS SECTIONS

INSIDE ENGINES

WIDE EYED EDITIONS

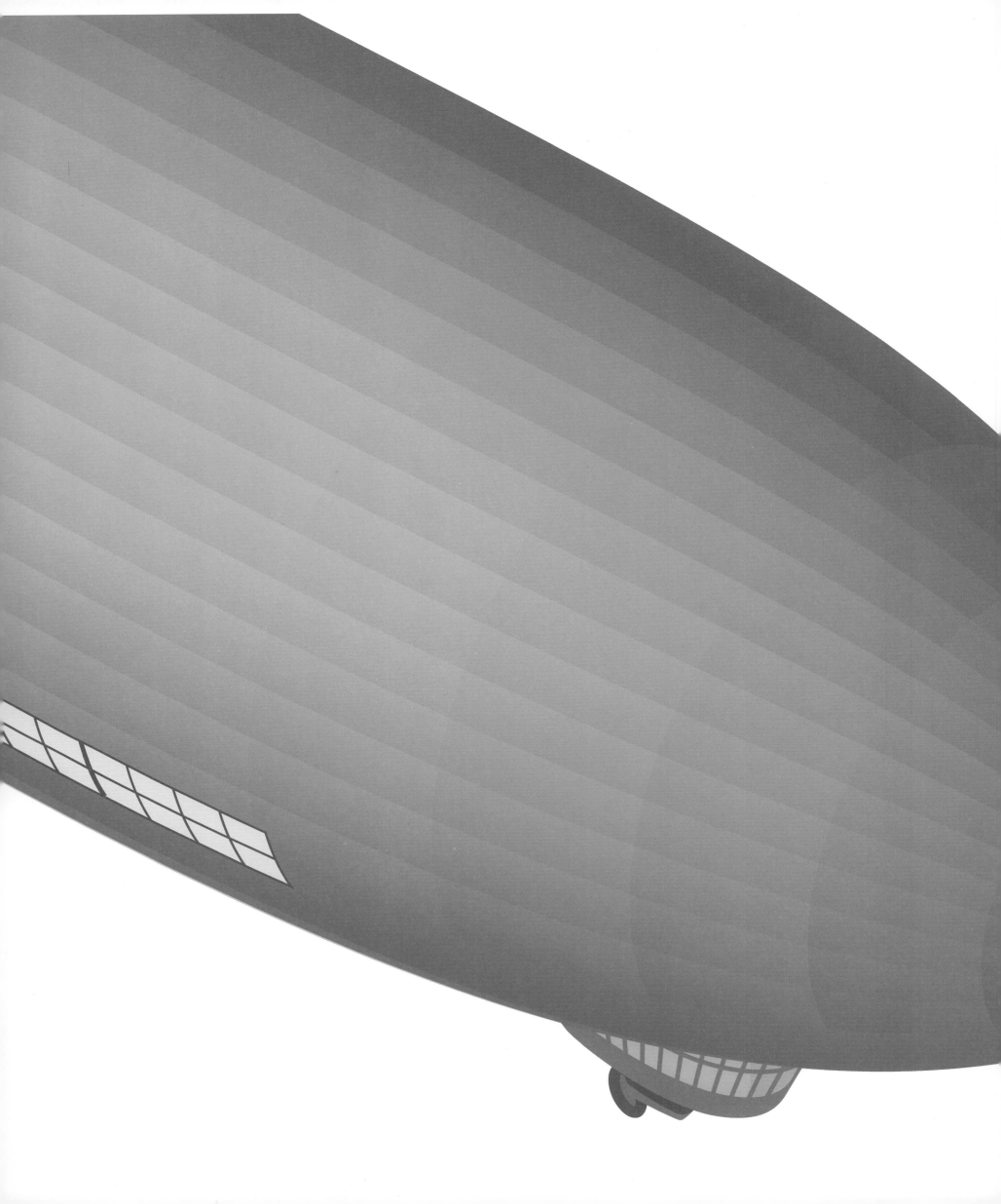

THROUGHOUT HISTORY, HUMANS HAVE INVENTED ALL KINDS
OF VEHICLES TO TRAVEL ACROSS LAND, SEA, AND AIR.

Every vehicle has a story hidden among its nuts and bolts.
Travel deep inside 15 supersize vehicles to discover their secrets
and get a glimpse of what life might be like on board.

What are you waiting for?

FASTEN YOUR SEAT BELTS
AND BON VOYAGE!

18TH CENTURY
ADVENTURE GALLEY

CAPTAINED BY THE FAMOUS PIRATE WILLIAM KIDD, THIS VERY LARGE SAILING SHIP IS KNOWN AS A GALLEY AND WAS USED FOR BATTLES.

01 Crew
The crew was made up of 150 men, including some convicts who were forced to work there. In 1697, the crew mutinied (revolted) because Kidd was not attacking enough ships! Because of the complaints from his men, he started to attack every ship that crossed their path, becoming a feared outlaw. Kidd was eventually captured and was hanged in 1701 in London.

02 Cannons
The ship had 34 cannons that each shot 11-pound balls, which could cause considerable damage. However, it wasn't a pirate's goal to sink ships—instead they wanted to steal riches! They would always try to make their victims surrender without a fight by firing warning shots into the water.

03 Helmsman
As wheel rudders had not yet been invented, in order to steer the ship, the helmsman directed the "tiller"—a long wooden rod connected to the rudder. To navigate, they used nautical charts and special instruments, such as a compass or an astrolabe.

04 Leading seaman
The leading seaman was the captain's right-hand man. They gave the crew their orders, especially during battles, and gave out punishments to anyone who disobeyed directions.

The Union Jack
At the service of the king of England, *Adventure Galley* flew the Union Jack high above the ship.

Captain's quarters
Captain Kidd had his own cabin, while the rest of the crew slept below deck in hammocks.

Rowboat
This little boat transported the crew to and from the shore.

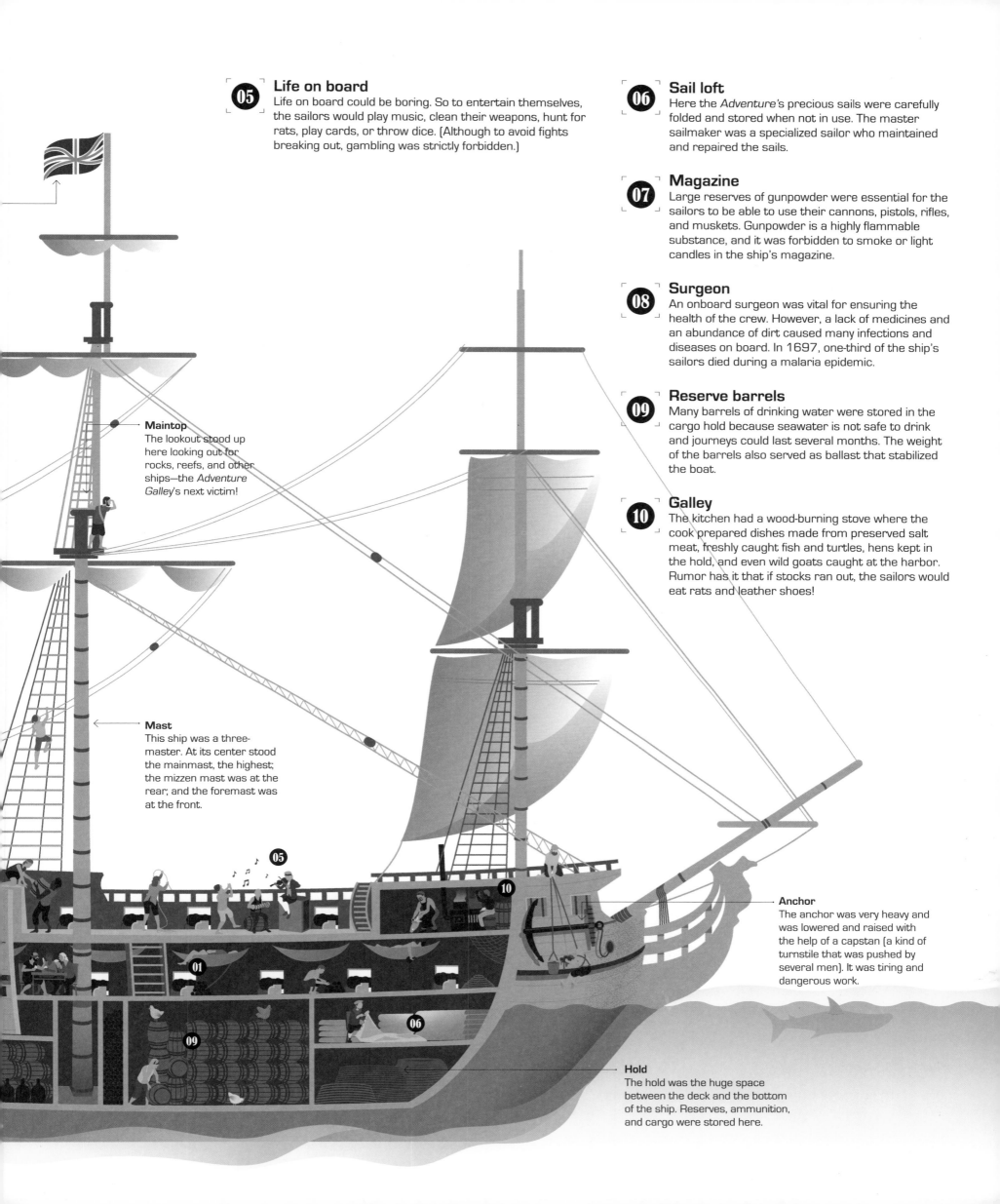

05 Life on board
Life on board could be boring. So to entertain themselves, the sailors would play music, clean their weapons, hunt for rats, play cards, or throw dice. (Although to avoid fights breaking out, gambling was strictly forbidden.)

06 Sail loft
Here the *Adventure*'s precious sails were carefully folded and stored when not in use. The master sailmaker was a specialized sailor who maintained and repaired the sails.

07 Magazine
Large reserves of gunpowder were essential for the sailors to be able to use their cannons, pistols, rifles, and muskets. Gunpowder is a highly flammable substance, and it was forbidden to smoke or light candles in the ship's magazine.

08 Surgeon
An onboard surgeon was vital for ensuring the health of the crew. However, a lack of medicines and an abundance of dirt caused many infections and diseases on board. In 1697, one-third of the ship's sailors died during a malaria epidemic.

09 Reserve barrels
Many barrels of drinking water were stored in the cargo hold because seawater is not safe to drink and journeys could last several months. The weight of the barrels also served as ballast that stabilized the boat.

10 Galley
The kitchen had a wood-burning stove where the cook prepared dishes made from preserved salt meat, freshly caught fish and turtles, hens kept in the hold, and even wild goats caught at the harbor. Rumor has it that if stocks ran out, the sailors would eat rats and leather shoes!

Maintop
The lookout stood up here looking out for rocks, reefs, and other ships—the *Adventure Galley*'s next victim!

Mast
This ship was a three-master. At its center stood the mainmast, the highest; the mizzen mast was at the rear; and the foremast was at the front.

Anchor
The anchor was very heavy and was lowered and raised with the help of a capstan (a kind of turnstile that was pushed by several men). It was tiring and dangerous work.

Hold
The hold was the huge space between the deck and the bottom of the ship. Reserves, ammunition, and cargo were stored here.

THE ORIENT EXPRESS

A TRUE PALACE ON TRACKS, THIS LUXURY TRAIN TRAVELED ALL THE WAY ACROSS EUROPE TO THE ORIENT.

Restaurant car
Three restaurant cars were open to guests, and each was as impressive as the last. Each one was decked out with silver cutlery, crystal glassware, and the finest of china. The famous glass designer René Lalique was commissioned to decorate the dining car's walls with intricate glass panelling. Lalique also contributed to other carriages, using the finest of enamels, leather, horn, and lacquer. His style is typical of the "art nouveau" movement.

Locomotive
The 230 G 353 locomotive is a celebrity in railway history. Built in France in 1922, it powered the *Orient Express* (and other famous trains) until 1970. It worked by using high-pressure steam—a bit like a pressure cooker. It was inspected regularly to ensure that it did not leak water and that everything was in working order.

Platform
There are small 3-foot square platforms between the train carriages that the railway workers used for breaks and fresh air.

Kitchen
Each meal served on the *Express* was prepared by a team of professional chefs, using a wood-fired oven. On the menu there might be red mullet, watercress soup, mashed potatoes, or chocolate torte—always served with champagne! Legend has it that a demanding passenger once asked for some gooseberry sauce to accompany his meat. When the kitchen announced they didn't have any, the conductor quickly hopped off the train during a stopover to buy some!

Conductor
Because the journey lasted four days, the train needed more than one conductor. A team of conductors rotated in shifts along the way. In 1901, the *Express*'s brakes failed while coming into Frankfurt station and the conductor responded too slowly. As a result, the train finally rolled to a stop inside the station restaurant! Fortunately, no one was injured.

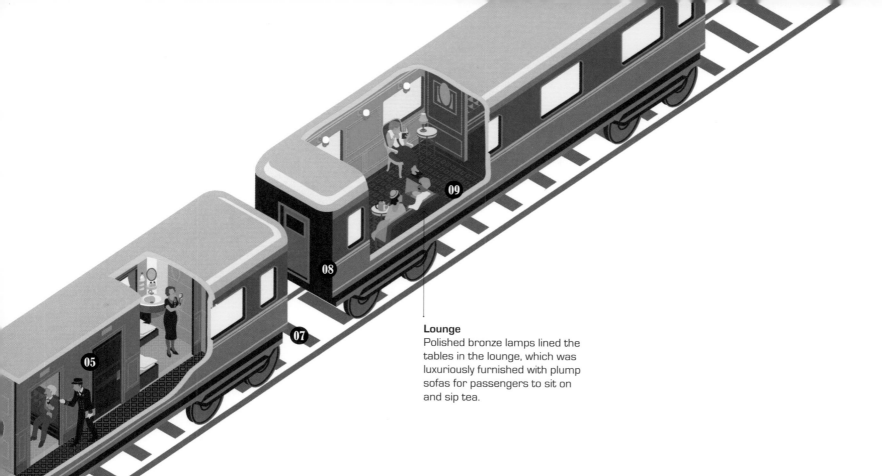

Lounge
Polished bronze lamps lined the tables in the lounge, which was luxuriously furnished with plump sofas for passengers to sit on and sip tea.

Sleeping car
When it was designed, the sleeping car was considered the epitome of modern design. Each compartment contained two beds made up with silk sheets, en-suite bathrooms, marble basins, central heating, and personalized dressing gowns. To call the bellboy, guests pressed a brass button.

 A long trip
To get from Paris to Istanbul, in Turkey, the *Orient Express* traveled 2,000 miles. It was relatively slow and could only travel around 30 and 60 miles per hour, making several stops along the way. This journey took around four days and four nights, which in the 19th century was actually record-breaking!

 The route
The *Orient Express*'s route frequently changed to form different journeys across a vast network of international stops. Sometimes starting from Lausanne (Switzerland), Venice, Verona, and Milan (Italy), Zagreb (Croatia), or Sofia (Bulgaria), it might eventually terminate in Beirut (Lebanon), Baghdad (Iraq), Cairo, Luxor, or Aswan (Egypt). During wars, the route was altered to avoid the countries where there was conflict.

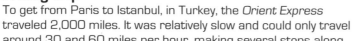 **Passengers**
Passengers of all ages came from across the world to travel on the *Orient Express*. Famous guests included the writer Graham Greene, the film stars Marlene Dietrich and Jean Gabin, the musician Josephine Baker, the scientist Albert Einstein, and even the secret agent Mata Hari.

 A magical journey
For four days, the passengers lived in close quarters. Given the small amount of space on board, there was nowhere to hide and often friendships and romances blossomed...
Europeans headed off to discover Asia and the East, while people from Asia went to discover Europe. Thanks to the *Orient Express*, the two sides of the world could meet.

 Controller
Just like today, the railway controller patrolled the train to ensure that the journey went smoothly. In Agatha Christie's famous novel *Murder on the Orient Express*, a murder takes place and a mystery controller with a woman's voice drifts up and down the train...

 Staff
Available at any time of the day, the onboard staff maintained the cabins, changed the sheets daily, served in the restaurants, and managed the provisions. Phew!

 Danger!
In 1891, a group of bandits jumped on the train and stole over $100,000—a fortune at the time. Later, in 1931, a Hungarian terrorist blew up a bridge near Budapest, derailing the train and killing 20 people. Then, in 1929, near Istanbul, ice on the tracks kept the *Express* at a standstill for five days! It was 15 degrees Fahrenheit in the cabins and the whole train was freezing!

 Carriages
Before World War I, the train cars were built out of teak, an expensive tropical wood, but after 1920, the frames were made of metal to stop the unpleasant cracking sound that the wood made on journeys. The cars were 56 feet long and were heated by steam, gas-lit, and very comfortable.

 Extravagance
In 1907, the maharajah of Cooch Behar state, a wealthy traveler, had his suite and carriage decorated in an Indian design. So that his wife did not catch a cold, he made the train stop in the heart of Bulgaria to purchase furs for her. As a thank-you, he presented the *Orient Express* staff with fine jewels.

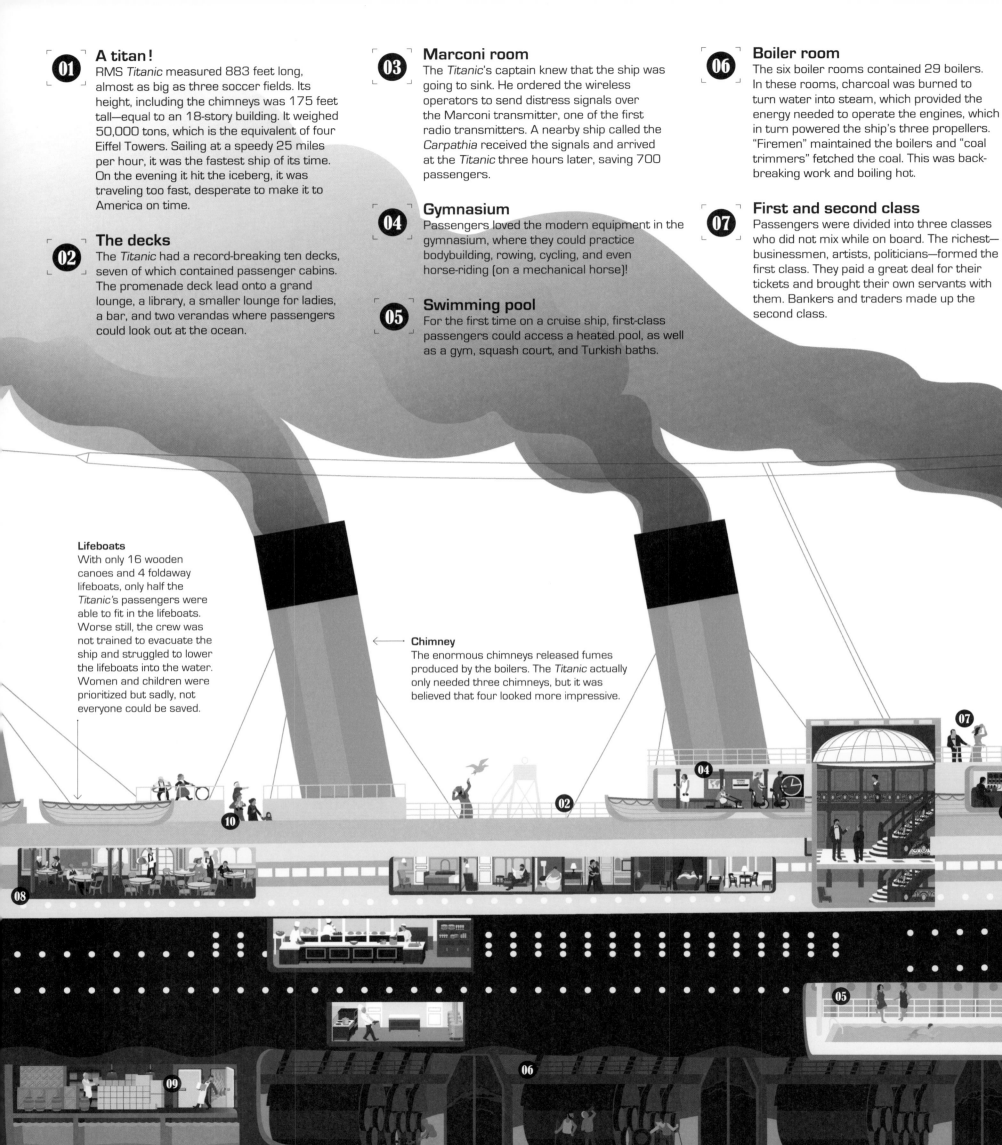

01 A titan!
RMS *Titanic* measured 883 feet long, almost as big as three soccer fields. Its height, including the chimneys was 175 feet tall—equal to an 18-story building. It weighed 50,000 tons, which is the equivalent of four Eiffel Towers. Sailing at a speedy 25 miles per hour, it was the fastest ship of its time. On the evening it hit the iceberg, it was traveling too fast, desperate to make it to America on time.

02 The decks
The *Titanic* had a record-breaking ten decks, seven of which contained passenger cabins. The promenade deck lead onto a grand lounge, a library, a smaller lounge for ladies, a bar, and two verandas where passengers could look out at the ocean.

03 Marconi room
The *Titanic*'s captain knew that the ship was going to sink. He ordered the wireless operators to send distress signals over the Marconi transmitter, one of the first radio transmitters. A nearby ship called the *Carpathia* received the signals and arrived at the *Titanic* three hours later, saving 700 passengers.

04 Gymnasium
Passengers loved the modern equipment in the gymnasium, where they could practice bodybuilding, rowing, cycling, and even horse-riding (on a mechanical horse)!

05 Swimming pool
For the first time on a cruise ship, first-class passengers could access a heated pool, as well as a gym, squash court, and Turkish baths.

06 Boiler room
The six boiler rooms contained 29 boilers. In these rooms, charcoal was burned to turn water into steam, which provided the energy needed to operate the engines, which in turn powered the ship's three propellers. "Firemen" maintained the boilers and "coal trimmers" fetched the coal. This was back-breaking work and boiling hot.

07 First and second class
Passengers were divided into three classes who did not mix while on board. The richest—businessmen, artists, politicians—formed the first class. They paid a great deal for their tickets and brought their own servants with them. Bankers and traders made up the second class.

Lifeboats
With only 16 wooden canoes and 4 foldaway lifeboats, only half the *Titanic*'s passengers were able to fit in the lifeboats. Worse still, the crew was not trained to evacuate the ship and struggled to lower the lifeboats into the water. Women and children were prioritized but sadly, not everyone could be saved.

Chimney
The enormous chimneys released fumes produced by the boilers. The *Titanic* actually only needed three chimneys, but it was believed that four looked more impressive.

08 Restaurant

Reserved for first class passengers, the restaurant served decadent food (with caviar, lobster, and quail often on the menu), while a live orchestra performed for the enjoyment of the guests. Following the collision, the orchestra carried on playing in an attempt to keep the passengers calm.

09 Food stores

Imagine the amount of food needed to feed everyone on board the *Titanic*! Its shopping list included: 25,000 pounds of poultry, 40,000 eggs, 7,000 heads of lettuce, 2,000 pounds of coffee, 15,000 bottles of beer, 10,000 pounds of sugar, and 1,200 quarts of ice cream.

10 Third class

The third class was formed of immigrants from over 40 different countries. They hoped they would find a better life in America, but sadly three-quarters of them never made it and died in the *Titanic* tragedy.

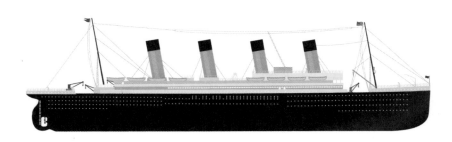

1912

RMS TITANIC

BUILT TO BE THE GREATEST PASSENGER LINER IN THE WORLD, THE RMS TITANIC WAS MADE FAMOUS AFTER ITS MAIDEN VOYAGE ENDED IN DISASTER WHEN IT STRUCK AN ICEBERG...

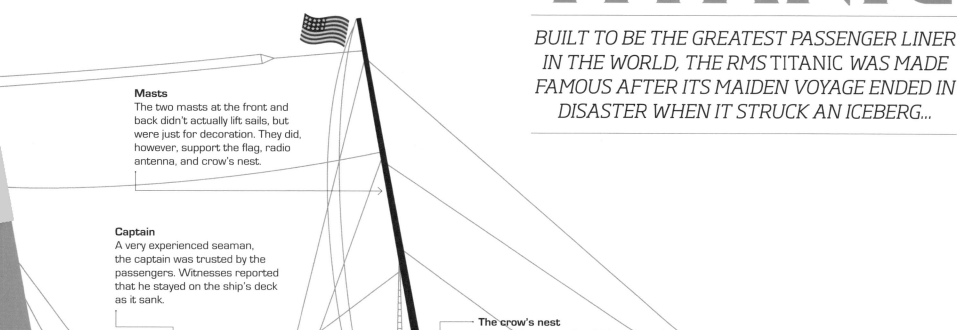

Masts
The two masts at the front and back didn't actually lift sails, but were just for decoration. They did, however, support the flag, radio antenna, and crow's nest.

Captain
A very experienced seaman, the captain was trusted by the passengers. Witnesses reported that he stayed on the ship's deck as it sank.

The crow's nest
This platform was the ship's observation point. On the evening of April 14, the fog obscured the watchman's vision, so he didn't see the approaching iceberg until it was too late.

Hull
Made of steel, the hull was solid with a double bottom and 16 watertight compartments. Nevertheless, the iceberg still managed to tear through the hull in six places.

1937

LZ 129
HINDENBURG
ZEPPELIN

THIS AIRSHIP, OR DIRIGIBLE BALLOON, WAS A GIANT OF THE SKY. HOWEVER, ITS DESTINY ENDED IN DISASTER...

 Metal structure
The skeleton-like frame was made out of duralumin, a light and strong alloy metal. The frame was made up of 15 rings that were connected by girders. In the center, a long corridor allowed the crew to move around the airship. The *Hindenburg* had two levels: the upper deck was called Deck A and contained the passenger cabin, while the lower deck, Deck B, accommodated the crew and kitchens. A bridge connected the two floors.

 The team
There were 61 crew members: officers, mechanics, an engineer, cooks, a dozen air stewards, maids who looked after the passengers, and even a postman! The crew slept in bunk beds at the rear of the lower deck while officers and captains had their own cabins.

 Gigantic
The airship's aerodynamic shape ressembled a missile. Measuring 803 feet long, it was more than three times the size of a Boeing 747, one of the largest airliners in the world! It was 144 feet high and could fit a 15-story building inside of it.

 Keel
A triangular keel formed the bottom structure of the ship. It contained the fuel tanks (kerosene) and ballast bags, each holding between 150 and 250 gallons of water. When the water was partially emptied, the airship became lighter and so rose in the air.

 Commander
The commander was in charge of the zeppelin. They directed the crew, giving orders to the mechanics via telegraph and speaking to the riggers (the people who were in charge of the airship's mooring ropes) through a long tube. It was too dangerous to use a phone because electrical sparks could cause a fire.

 Passengers
Up to 72 passengers could travel on the airship. It was an expensive trip, but everyone loved the zeppelin's luxurious interiors and the sensation of floating high in the sky in peaceful silence.

D·LZ 129

Cover
The airship's frame was covered by a cotton canvas fabric so big it could cover five soccer fields! A varnished paint containing iron and aluminium powder sealed the canvas. This cover protected the ship from the sun's heat and rays, which prevented the gas balloons stored inside from overheating.

Propeller
Four propellers moved the airship in a horizontal direction. Each was powered by its own engine. The *Hindenburg* was not very fast, though, traveling at a maximum speed of 80 miles per hour. A trip from Germany to the East Coast of America took two and a half days—a trip that would take about 11 hours today!

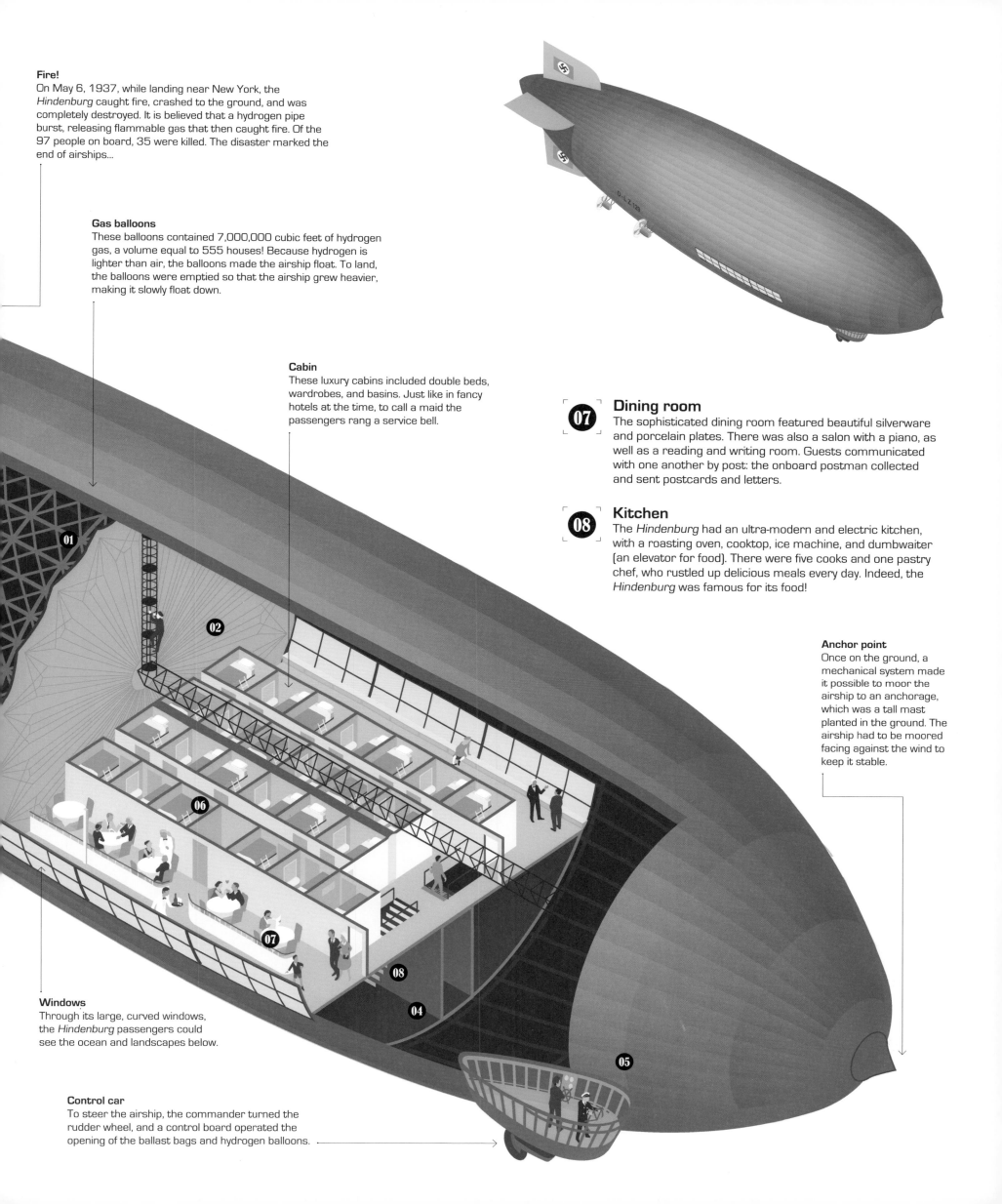

Fire!
On May 6, 1937, while landing near New York, the *Hindenburg* caught fire, crashed to the ground, and was completely destroyed. It is believed that a hydrogen pipe burst, releasing flammable gas that then caught fire. Of the 97 people on board, 35 were killed. The disaster marked the end of airships...

Gas balloons
These balloons contained 7,000,000 cubic feet of hydrogen gas, a volume equal to 555 houses! Because hydrogen is lighter than air, the balloons made the airship float. To land, the balloons were emptied so that the airship grew heavier, making it slowly float down.

Cabin
These luxury cabins included double beds, wardrobes, and basins. Just like in fancy hotels at the time, to call a maid the passengers rang a service bell.

07 Dining room
The sophisticated dining room featured beautiful silverware and porcelain plates. There was also a salon with a piano, as well as a reading and writing room. Guests communicated with one another by post: the onboard postman collected and sent postcards and letters.

08 Kitchen
The *Hindenburg* had an ultra-modern and electric kitchen, with a roasting oven, cooktop, ice machine, and dumbwaiter (an elevator for food). There were five cooks and one pastry chef, who rustled up delicious meals every day. Indeed, the *Hindenburg* was famous for its food!

Anchor point
Once on the ground, a mechanical system made it possible to moor the airship to an anchorage, which was a tall mast planted in the ground. The airship had to be moored facing against the wind to keep it stable.

Windows
Through its large, curved windows, the *Hindenburg* passengers could see the ocean and landscapes below.

Control car
To steer the airship, the commander turned the rudder wheel, and a control board operated the opening of the ballast bags and hydrogen balloons.

Armor
The tank was covered in steel armor. However, in some places it was too thin to resist the enemy's anti-tank shells. To further protect the tank, the crew attached steel patches on top of the armor.

Ammunition
If an enemy missile pierced the tank's armor, its own ammunition could explode and harm the men inside. It was a very dangerous job.

Gun turret
This rotating turret allowed the tank crew to monitor their surroundings from all sides (although this did then expose them to enemy fire). In battle, the turret hatch was closed and the crew had to navigate using a periscope.

Caterpillar tracks
These tracks spread the tank's weight over a large surface area, which decreased its pressure on the ground and enabled it to drive quickly across almost every surface (except over very soft ground or big rocks).

20th CENTURY

M4A4 SHERMAN
TANK

THIS AMERICAN ARMORED FIGHTING VEHICLE–OR TANK–WAS A CELEBRITY DURING WORLD WAR II.

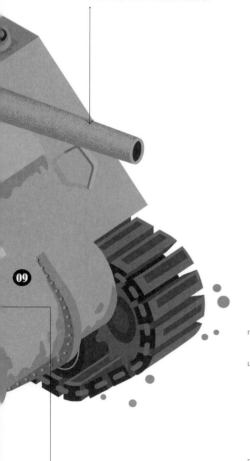

Armament
This gun fired shells at enemy tanks, light vehicles, and soldiers. Its diameter was 75 millimeters. Nowadays, tank guns have a higher caliber diameter of around 120 millimeters.

Machine gun
The Sherman M4A4 was also equipped with two secondary armament machine guns, and sometimes even a third on its turret.

 Tank driver
It's harder to drive a tank than a car, but it's still easier than flying a plane! The tank driver had to use two gears—each controlling one of the tracks. To turn left, the driver pulled on the right lever, and to brake, they lifted their foot off the pedals. They were often helped by an assistant driver.

 Heavyweight
The Sherman M4A4 weighed around 33 tons, which is as much as 15 cars. It was so heavy it could actually crush a car! However, its weight also slowed it down and it could only travel at around 22 miles per hour.

 Inside
There wasn't much room inside the tank. It was very dark and the engines roared loudly. This made the exchanges between crew members very difficult and they often communicated with hand gestures instead.

 Too high
The Sherman M4A4, a medium tank, measured 19 feet long, 8.5 feet wide, and 9 feet high. Its above-average height posed a problem: it was easily identifiable by enemy forces.

 Tank crew
The tank crew was made up of five members: the gunner, the loader, the driver, the assistant driver, and the commander. The latter directed the group, giving orders for actions, movements, or shots.

 Safety hatch
In case of fire, an additional hatch at the base of the tank allowed the crew to quickly evacuate the vehicle. However, the hatch was so narrow that most crew members would have had a hard time fitting through!

 Ventilator
When the tank was completely sealed, a fresh air supply was pumped inside using a ventilation system. This air also helped to cool down the engine, and pumped out any harmful fumes that might have been produced inside the tank.

 Periscope
With the aid of a periscope, the tank commander could survey their surroundings from a sheltered position. The periscope could rotate 360 degrees, offering a complete view of the area.

 Engine
The powerful Sherman engine, which was also used in planes and buses, was highly flammable, which earned it the nickname "the roast beef barbeque" among German soldiers.

SATURN V
ROCKET LAUNCHER

THIS ROCKET TRANSPORTED SATELLITES, PROBES, AND ASTRONAUTS INTO SPACE. IT WAS EVEN USED FOR THE APOLLO MOON LANDINGS!

04 Stabilizers
These fins, found at the rear of the fuselage (the body of the rocket), helped the rocket remain stable and on trajectory by preventing it from pitching.

05 First stage
The first stage, which contained the liquid oxygen tank, was only used for two minutes and 30 seconds after takeoff! It propelled the entire launcher into the air, before detaching and letting the second stage take over.

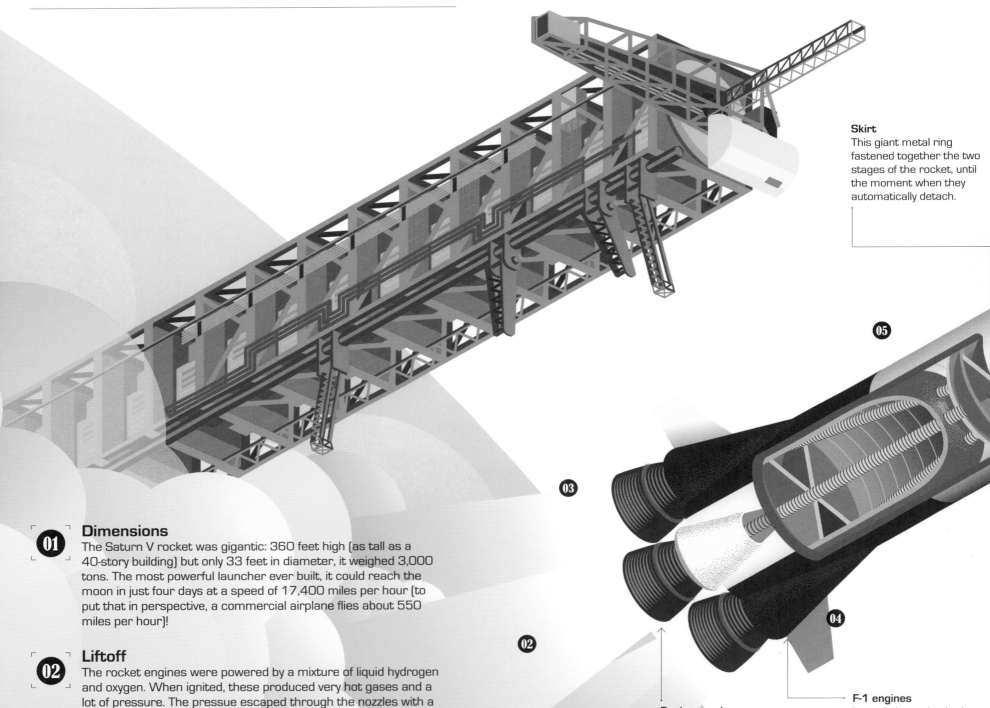

Skirt
This giant metal ring fastened together the two stages of the rocket, until the moment when they automatically detach.

01 Dimensions
The Saturn V rocket was gigantic: 360 feet high (as tall as a 40-story building) but only 33 feet in diameter, it weighed 3,000 tons. The most powerful launcher ever built, it could reach the moon in just four days at a speed of 17,400 miles per hour (to put that in perspective, a commercial airplane flies about 550 miles per hour)!

02 Liftoff
The rocket engines were powered by a mixture of liquid hydrogen and oxygen. When ignited, these produced very hot gases and a lot of pressure. The pressue escaped through the nozzles with a phenomenal force, which pushed the rocket off the ground.

03 Launch day
On launch day, the tension was high both on board and on the ground, among staff in the control center. It was the culmination of several years of preparation and intense work. Everything was calculated within a millimeter of precision—there was absolutely no room for error when the lives of astronauts were at stake.

Engine nozzles
These ducts, located at the rear of the first stage engines, allowed hot gases, produced through combustion, to escape and propel the rocket forward. Jet airplanes possess similar nozzles.

F-1 engines
In total, the rocket had 11 gas-generator F-1 engines. Each stage was autonomous and had its own motors and fuel reservoir. The first and second stages had five engines between them.

Lunar module
Eagle, the Apollo 11 lunar module (or LM), was the small spacecraft that landed on the moon under the guidance of two astronauts, including the mission commander. The LM contained all the scientific equipment that was needed to study the moon, as well as a lunar rover, a small practical all-terrain buggy for getting around.

Instrument unit
This compartment houses most of the guidance, electronic, and location systems. The rocket is neither controlled by groundstaff nor by astronauts: it is fully automated!

06

Launch escape system
This arrow-shaped device ensured the safety of astronauts. On Earth during the launch, there was a risk that the rocket could explode during takeoff. If this had happened, the escape capsule would have detached from the rocket and immediately moved the passengers a safe distance away from the rocket before lowering them with parachutes.

01

10

08

11

07

09

 Moon mission
Once on the moon, the Apollo mission astronauts collected rock samples and conducted experiments—like detecting cosmic rays—using scientific equiment. They walked on the lunar soil (an event filmed and broadcast live across the world), where they planted the American flag.

 Payload
At the top of the rocket is the "payload." This small component was the most important part of the rocket. It was ejected upward by the thrust of the first- and second-stage engines and eventually ended up in space carrying a satellite, a probe, or a space capsule and crew.

 Wonder
From their capsule, the astronauts could see the tiny blue planet Earth surrounded by immense outer space.

 Second stage
The second stage, containing the liquid hydrogen tank, was used for six minutes. It allowed the launcher to reach an altitude of 115 miles and a speed of 15,300 miles per hour.

 Command module
While two astronauts explored the lunar surface, the third stayed with the spacecraft as it orbited around the moon. After 21 hours, the upper part of the LM took off and rejoined the control module for the team to return to Earth together.

 Space sickness
In theory, astronauts should have perfect physical and mental health before heading into space. But during the missions, some suffer from space sickness. This is a kind of motion sickness that causes nausea and vomiting. If an astronaut has a bad cold or a fever, the mission is postponed.

 USA
The United States of America and the Soviet Union (which became Russia) were once in fierce competition to get into space first. The Americans were the first to get to the moon in 1969, but the Soviets were the first to send a man into space in 1963!

12

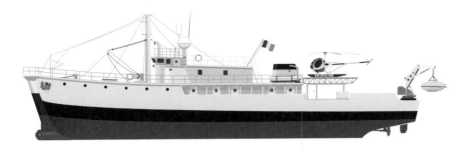

20TH CENTURY

R.V. CALYPSO

THIS WORLD-FAMOUS RESEARCH VESSEL WAS DEDICATED TO SCIENTIFIC AND OCEANOGRAPHIC RESEARCH.

Radar
The naval radar emits electromagnetic currents that could detect obstacles in the ocean, like icebergs or other ships.

Viewing platform
This 10-foot long platform was added to the bow (the front) of the *Calypso* to film the dolphins that often swim alongside the ship.

04

05

01

Glass observation chamber
Located 10 feet below the waterline, this chamber was equipped with five portholes where you could film exceptional underwater shots!

Hull
The *Calypso* was a former minesweeping ship, so its hull was made out of wood and was very solid. The ship had a low draft, which meant it could float high in the water and allowed the ship to venture into shallow water without running aground.

Lodgings
These simple cabins containing bunkbeds are where the team slept.

Scientists
Oceanographers and zoologists study the behavior of sea lions or sharks. New species were even discovered while on board the *Calypso*.

 Crew
Thirty people made up the crew of the ship, including: sailors, cameramen, sound engineers, electricians, photographers, divers, mechanics, radio operators, and a cook! The teams varied according to each mission.

 Captain Cousteau
A navy officer, Jacques-Yves Cousteau was captain of the ship. He is known for being passionate about the underwater world and his documentary films and commitment to the environment have made him famous across the world. Nicknamed "le Pasha," meaning "the skipper," Cousteau is instantly recognizable by his bright red hat.

 Danger!
The *Calypso* faced many dangers, like cyclones, storms, running into sandbanks, and even hitting an iceberg.

 The factory
This part of the ship's hull, also known as "the factory," is where much of the work was done. It was made up of two engine compressors, a mechanical workshop, refrigerated lockers, and three laboratories, including one that was air-conditioned so that chemical reactions could be carried out in a controlled environment.

 Underwater cameraman
It might seem a little claustrophobic for a cameraman to be locked underwater in this tiny submarine, but it contained enough oxygen for 24 hours and it remained in radio contact with the vessel at all times. In case of an emergency, a second submarine could attach itself onto the first, lifting it to the surface.

 Underwater scooter
Most marine life can swim faster than humans. In order to film alongside them, Cousteau's team invented sea scooters that can propel a cameraman through the ocean at 3 miles per hour.

Captain's quarters
The captain slept here, separate from the rest of the team. The famous captain Jacques-Yves Cousteau lead the *Calypso*'s many succesful expeditions.

"The square"
This is where the team ate together. To let everyone know that food was ready, a bell was rung.

Helicopter
The ship's helipad could accommodate a small helicopter to ensure constant contact with land.

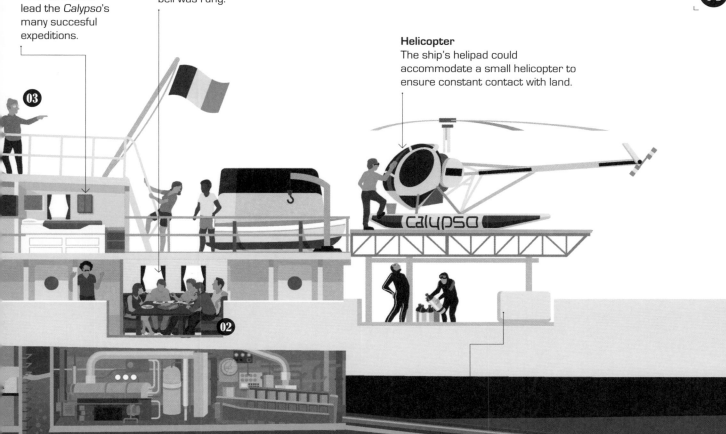

Moon pool
Through the kitchen, a "moon pool" was built that created an opening into the ship's hull to give direct access to the sea for scuba divers. Don't worry—it closed securely with a special seal!

Divers
Divers explored wrecks and filmed marine life. They worked as a team and were often volunteers on the *Calypso*. It was a risky job and there were some fatal accidents, but these people were passionate about their work.

Cameraman
In 1953, the onboard team developed new cameras and electronic flashes that work underwater. Thanks to them, it is now possible to see and film marine animals in their natural habitat.

Engine room
The boat's two powerful engines were stored here. They can carry the *Calypso*'s 400 tons of weight at a speed of 10 knots (11 miles per hour)!

Mini-submarine
These speedy little submarines were hand-operated by a driver lying on their stomach. They were equipped with arms that could collect samples, a camera, and a film recorder. Their small size (3 feet by 6 feet) earned them the nickname "the sea flea."

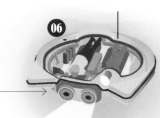

Diving saucer
The SP-350 Denise or "diving saucer" could fit two people in it and travel up to 1,300 feet underwater for 4 hours. It was propelled by a jet of water that helped it navigate around.

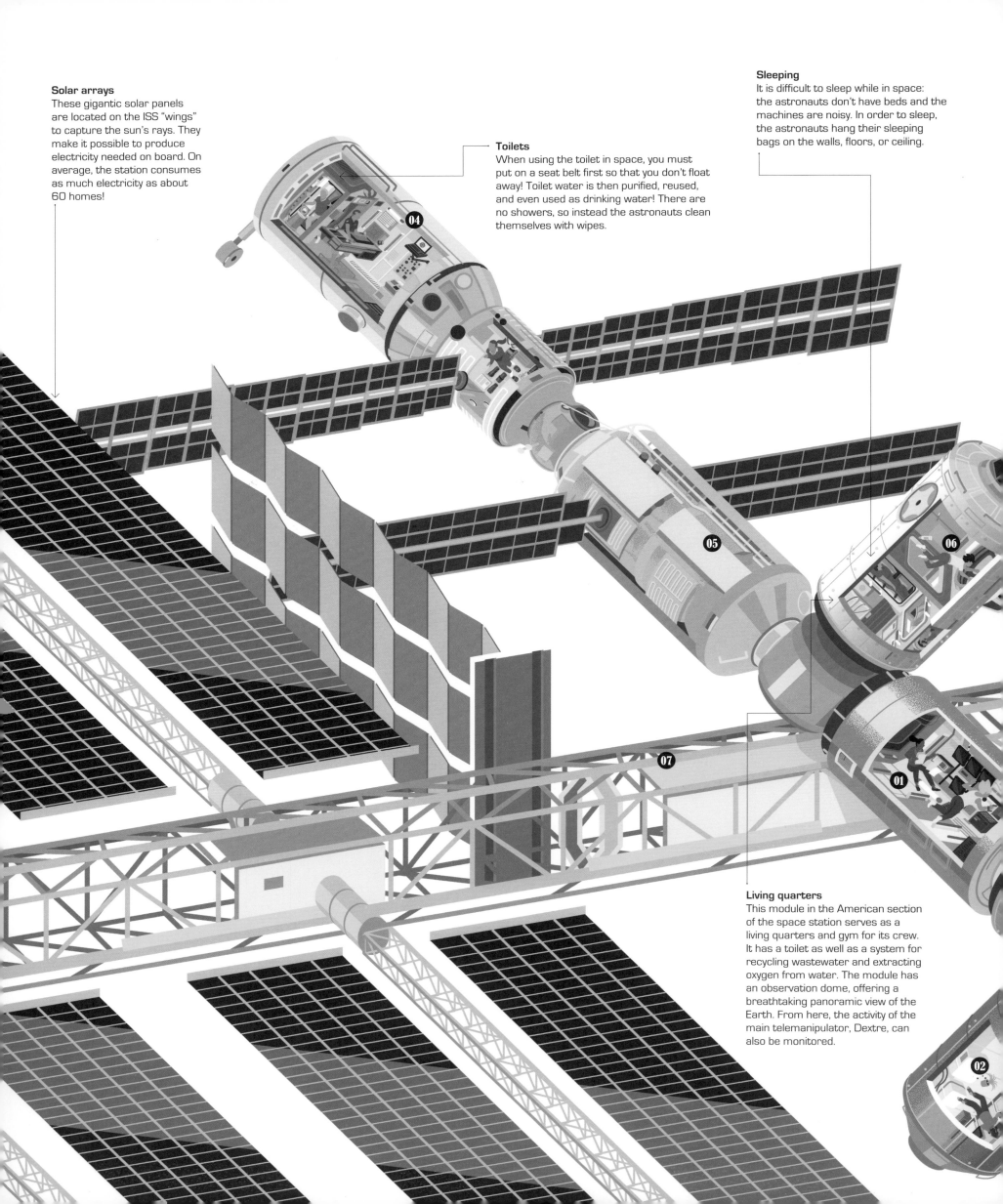

Solar arrays
These gigantic solar panels are located on the ISS "wings" to capture the sun's rays. They make it possible to produce electricity needed on board. On average, the station consumes as much electricity as about 60 homes!

Toilets
When using the toilet in space, you must put on a seat belt first so that you don't float away! Toilet water is then purified, reused, and even used as drinking water! There are no showers, so instead the astronauts clean themselves with wipes.

Sleeping
It is difficult to sleep while in space: the astronauts don't have beds and the machines are noisy. In order to sleep, the astronauts hang their sleeping bags on the walls, floors, or ceiling.

Living quarters
This module in the American section of the space station serves as a living quarters and gym for its crew. It has a toilet as well as a system for recycling wastewater and extracting oxygen from water. The module has an observation dome, offering a breathtaking panoramic view of the Earth. From here, the activity of the main telemanipulator, Dextre, can also be monitored.

Destiny

Also known as the United States laboratory, this lab is concerned with the effects of living in space on the human body. It has a porthole facing planet Earth: a view like no other!

Columbus

In the European laboratory, research is focused on biology, in particular on how humans can adapt to space environments with zero gravity (gravity is the force that attracts everything to the Earth's center and gives objects weight). Research in physics, material sciences, meteorology, and astronomy also take place here.

Kibo

Like the other modules, Kibo is pressurized using a system that keeps the air pressure and supply constant. This is because at high altitudes, atmospheric pressure (the force exerted by the mixture of gases that make up the Earth's atmosphere) decreases so much that humans could not survive.

20TH CENTURY (1998)

INTERNATIONAL SPACE STATION

THIS GIANT SPACE LABORATORY ORBITS AROUND PLANET EARTH AND IS HOME TO AN INTERNATIONAL TEAM OF ASTRONAUTS.

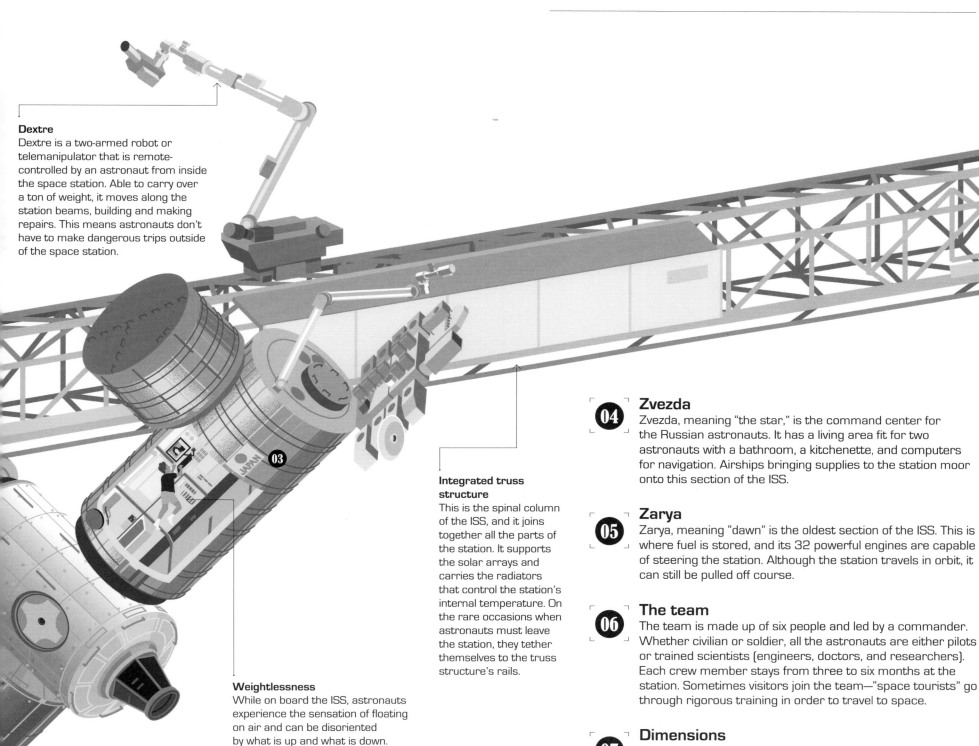

Dextre

Dextre is a two-armed robot or telemanipulator that is remote-controlled by an astronaut from inside the space station. Able to carry over a ton of weight, it moves along the station beams, building and making repairs. This means astronauts don't have to make dangerous trips outside of the space station.

Integrated truss structure

This is the spinal column of the ISS, and it joins together all the parts of the station. It supports the solar arrays and carries the radiators that control the station's internal temperature. On the rare occasions when astronauts must leave the station, they tether themselves to the truss structure's rails.

Weightlessness

While on board the ISS, astronauts experience the sensation of floating on air and can be disoriented by what is up and what is down. Weightlessness can cause "space sickness," which makes astronauts feel tired and nauseous.

Zvezda

Zvezda, meaning "the star," is the command center for the Russian astronauts. It has a living area fit for two astronauts with a bathroom, a kitchenette, and computers for navigation. Airships bringing supplies to the station moor onto this section of the ISS.

Zarya

Zarya, meaning "dawn" is the oldest section of the ISS. This is where fuel is stored, and its 32 powerful engines are capable of steering the station. Although the station travels in orbit, it can still be pulled off course.

The team

The team is made up of six people and led by a commander. Whether civilian or soldier, all the astronauts are either pilots or trained scientists (engineers, doctors, and researchers). Each crew member stays from three to six months at the station. Sometimes visitors join the team—"space tourists" go through rigorous training in order to travel to space.

Dimensions

The ISS is the biggest space station ever built: it is as long as a soccer field (360 feet), as high as a 10-story building (100 feet), and weighs about 450 tons. Before it was built, only eight other stations existed: seven Russian (Salyut) and one American (Skylab).

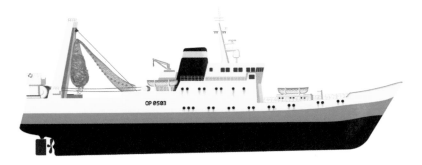

20TH CENTURY
FISHING
TRAWLER

THIS ENORMOUS INDUSTRIAL FISHING VESSEL IS LIKE A FACTORY THAT FLOATS ON WATER! THE FISH CAUGHT ON BOARD ARE IMMEDIATELY CLEANED, FROZEN, AND MADE READY TO EAT.

Deckhand
Deckhands are tasked with catching, sorting, cleaning, and freezing the fish. They also repair nets, service the ship, and do the cooking. It's hard work that needs to be done day and night.

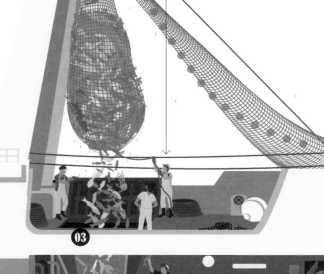

Trawl net
This huge net is in the shape of a pocket and is dragged behind the trawler by cables. The closed section is called the "cod-end," and its mesh size determines which fish are captured and which can escape. A system of remote-controlled chains and floats keep the net open when underwater as well as modifying its shape and depth. During the trawl, the fish are collected from the net every two hours.

Fish
Different nets are used to capture specific varieties of fish: sole, skate, and langoustine are found at the bottom of the sea; while tuna, sea bream, sea bass, and anchovies swim closer to the surface. Trawling techniques are now so effective that fishermen have been criticized for "overfishing," which is when too many fish are caught, resulting in the fish population being reduced. To protect endangered species of fish, quotas have been introduced so that trawlers can only capture a certain number of them.

01 Dimensions

A large trawler is about 160 feet long, which is roughly the same as four buses. Some giant trawlers can even measure double that!

02 Weather conditions

In a strong storm, it's not safe for the trawler to set sail. However, if the sea is too calm and there are no fish, then the sailors get bored!

03 Trapdoor

From the net, the fish slide through this hatch and fall below the deck, where they are transported along conveyor belts to the workroom.

04 Life on board

It's not easy living on board a fishing trawler. The ship is noisy, bumpy, and waves constantly beat against the boat—fortunately, fishermen rarely get seasick! The deck can become very slippery, the wind can become very violent, and conditions are usually wet. Fishermen have to spend long periods of time away from their family, and there is always the risk of falling overboard or unearthing unexploded World War II missiles.

05 Fishing hoist

The hoist is a cylinder around which the cables that hold the trawling net are wound. It allows the net to be lowered and hoisted out of the water. Once hoisted out of the water and back on board, the net is opened and its contents of fish is emptied on to the deck.

06 Captain or "skipper"

The captain is an experienced seaman who is in charge of the crew and the catch. They control the boat and decide when the trawl net should be lowered back into the water. The captain knows the fishing grounds, seabed, safety rules, size, and species of fish better than anyone else on board.

07 Wheelhouse

From this cabin, the ship is steered. GPS and navigation software help to keep the trawler on the right route. A depth-finder calculates the distance between the bottom of the sea and the trawl net so that the net does not tear or get caught, while a sonar indicates the presence of a school of fish.

Bosun
The bosun is the captain's right-hand man. They delegate tasks to the deckhands and oversee any maneuvers that are needed on deck. The bosun launches and raises the trawling nets, while monitoring the quality and processing of the fish.

Lifeboat
Sometimes the trawler can hit a rock or a shipwreck. This tears the cables and unbalances the ship, which may begin to lean or "list" dangerously. The trawler might even capsize. If there is time, the crew will quickly jump into the lifeboats and escape to safety.

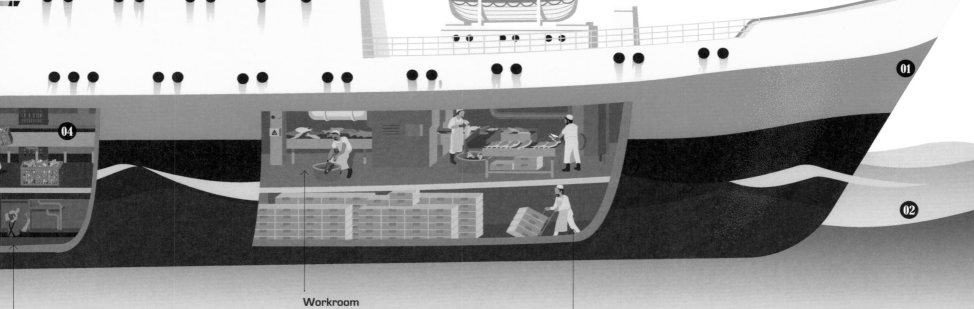

Mechanic
Essential to the smooth running of the trawler, the mechanic monitors the main and auxiliary engines. They must also regularly check the cooling systems because warm fish means lost money!

Workroom
In the workroom, using special machinery, the deckhands known as "slimers" clean the fish, cut them into long slices (fillets), pack them into boxes, and store them in cold chambers or freezers kept at minus 40 degrees Fahrenheit. In one day, up to 40 tons of fish can be caught and processed.

The holds
Under the deck, the holds are where the machines used to prepare and conserve the fish are kept. This is the "factory" of the trawler.

NUCLEAR-POWERED ATTACK SUBMARINE

THIS SUBMARINE IS A SPECIAL MILITARY VESSEL, IT PATROLS THE SURFACE AND THE DEPTHS OF OCEANS WITH THE UTMOST SECRECY.

Periscopes
The submarine's periscopes are like its eyes. Equipped with mirrors and lenses that are connected to a video camera, the periscopes peer up through the roof and can rotate. When on watch duty, the periscope allows the marines to scan a large expanse of ocean, and during an attack, it enables them to observe a close target.

Dormitories
The marines sleep in bunks. The lowest ranked sleep alongside 15 other men in cabins that are situated in the submarine's lower deck—in between the torpedoes! The commander has their own cabin.

Torpedoe tubes
These tubes launch torpedoes that each weigh around one ton. Equipped with an electric motor and an explosive charge, the torpedoes spin underwater at 40 miles per hour to sink their target, which can be about a mile away. This attack submarine doesn't carry any nuclear weapons. Instead, these are carried by ballistic missile submarines.

Sonar
Sonar can detect obstacles or ships underwater. It works by emitting very high-pitched sounds—called ultrasounds—that bounce off objects and are sent back to the submarine, like an echo. These sound waves can even indicate the position and distance of an obstacle!

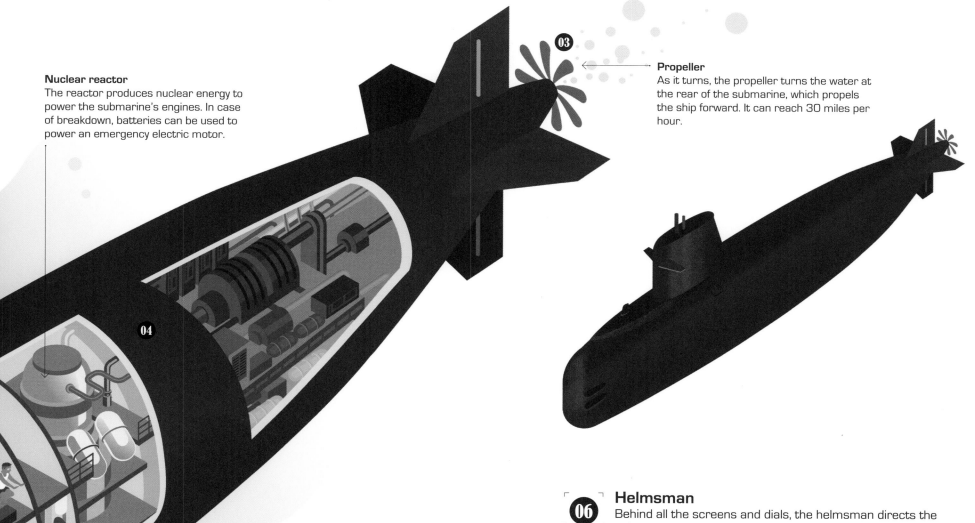

Nuclear reactor
The reactor produces nuclear energy to power the submarine's engines. In case of breakdown, batteries can be used to power an emergency electric motor.

Propeller
As it turns, the propeller turns the water at the rear of the submarine, which propels the ship forward. It can reach 30 miles per hour.

Lighting
When they're at the bottom of the sea, the crew can't distinguish between day and night. To make sure they keep the same rhythm as normal, the lighting of the submarine is varied: in daytime the light is yellow, while at night it is dim red.

Leisure time
Unsurprisingly, sometimes the marines on board get bored. To unwind, they watch movies and play games. To stay fit, there is exercise equipment on board—some submarines even have exercise bikes in the torpedo room!

Rudder
The helmsman directs the submarine using a remote rudder. This vertical plate acts like a fish tail, swiveling to the right or to the left, it changes the direction of the vessel.

No portholes!
There are no portholes to look out of and see underwater. Instead, the crew must blindly guide the submarine using instruments like sonar, antennae, periscopes, and naval maps.

Watertight compartments
A water leak or a fire is the biggest threat to a submarine. Fortunately, the submarine is divided into compartments that can each be closed and kept isolated to prevent water or fire from spreading. In an emergency, if the submarine is at a shallow depth, the crew is evacuated to the surface via an airlock.

Helmsman
Behind all the screens and dials, the helmsman directs the submarine up and down or left to right, controlling its pitch as it ascends and descends to keep it flat. If the submarine pitches, the marines could lose their footing and fall over!

Analysts
With computers connected to sonars, analysts observe the passage of ships. Some analysts are particularly good at detecting by sound whether a ship is a modern ferry, an old freighter, a submarine, or even a singing whale!

Crew
Around 70 people make up the crew, and as always in the military, each marine has a rank that corresponds to their function. In general, there are eight officers who are in charge, 52 non-commissioned officers (NCOs) and around ten quartermasters who work as helmsmen and senior staff. The rest of the crew are known as seamen.

Quarters
The marines work in shifts of four hours, called "quarters." They then rest for four hours and work again for another four hours. Sleeping in such short bursts and waking up just as your teammates go to bed can be very tiring indeed!

Nurse
The onboard nurse treats illnesses, small wounds, and toothaches. The medical professional is also responsible for checking the water and air and water quality.

Cafeteria
The cook packs enough food for the journey, and with the help of an assistant, they cook for all the crew. The kitchen is a tiny galley just 50 square feet and there is always a risk that the food will spill if the submarine suddenly dips! Mealtimes are a rare moment of relaxation, and the food is essential to keeping the crew nourished.

FIRE ENGINE

HERE COME THE FIREFIGHTERS! A FIRE ENGINE CONTAINS ALL THE NECESSARY EQUIPMENT TO GET A FIRE UNDER CONTROL QUICKLY AND RESCUE ANY VICTIMS.

Cabin
En route to the fire, the team of about four firefighters get ready in the cabin. They keep in radio contact with the emergency coordination center, who keeps them up-to-date on the progress of the incident.

Maps and building plans
To navigate the site of the fire, firefighters use GPS systems and street maps. The fire brigade also have access to water, gas, and electricity plans, which can help them to identify any nearby gas pipes that are at risk of exploding if reached by flames.

Turntable ladder
This big ladder completely unfolds in just one minute! Measuring between 80 and 160 feet, it allows firefighters to reach up ten floors of a building. The fire brigade can then enter a building through its windows to save anyone trapped inside and also attack the fire from above.

Revolving light
When the fire engine is on a mission, one or two blue lights flash to warn cars and passersby that there is an emergency and the vehicle has priority on the roads.

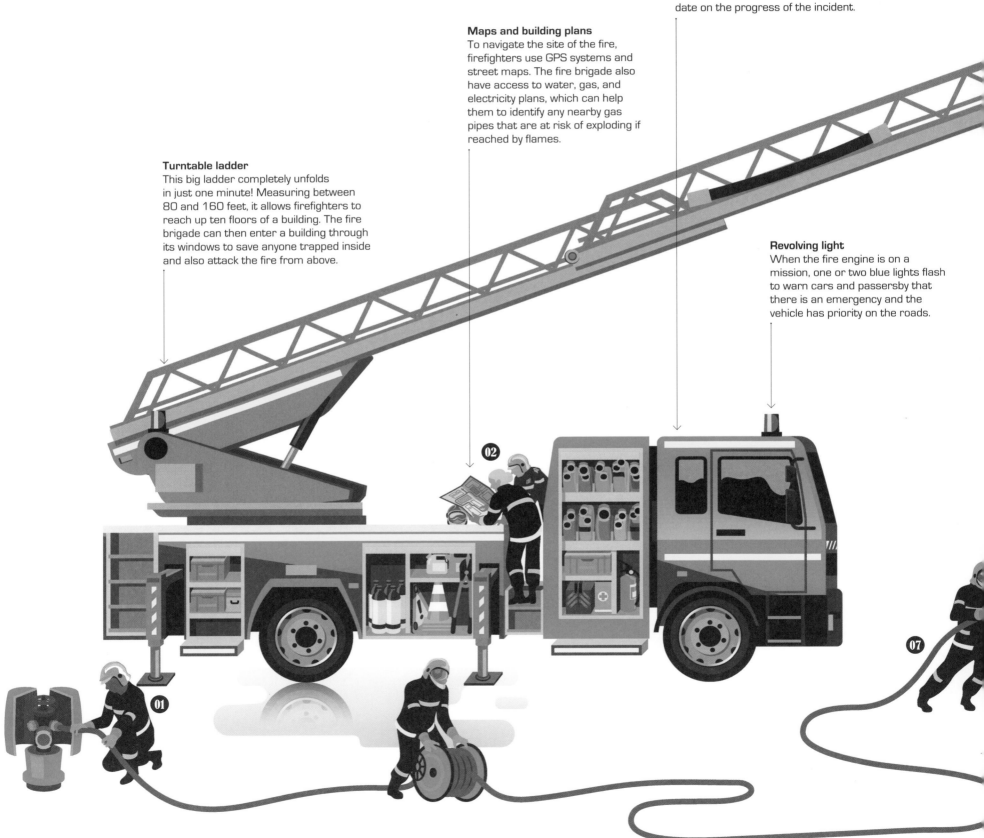

Basket
This raised platform can lift a fireman up into the air who then steers, raises, and elevates the ladder using a dashboard. The basket can also accommodate fire victims.

Water pump
The water is pumped at such a high pressure that the jet could knock a person down! If the fire is too strong, the water may evaporate in the heat. In these instances, the water is mixed with an emulsifier to create a foam that can stifle the fire.

 Volunteer firefighters
In most major towns and cities, firefighters are made up of a professional team. However, in more rural areas, they can be civilian volunteers who do other things as their main jobs.

 Firewomen
In the UK in 2016, only 5% of firefighters were women. However, the number is growing and many more women are employed as general support and fire control staff.

 Difficulties
Day and night, firefighters are ready to face the danger that their job entails. They must help people who are going through very difficult situations, supporting them, rescuing them, and providing first aid.

 Self-contained breathing apparatus
During a fire, toxic and deadly gases are released, like carbon monoxide. To avoid inhaling these, firefighters wear a mask attached to a bottle of compressed air carried on their backs. This special equiment can also detect if a firefighter has stopped moving, which might mean they are in danger.

 Uniform
A firefighter's uniform and gloves are fire retardant and have reflective tape that allow them to be seen, even in smoke. Their helmet protects their head and neck from falling debris and electrical sparks, while their belt carries a flashlight and a hydrant wrench, which is used to open doors without handles and fire hydrants.

 Cutting tools
An ax may be used to break down a locked door and rescue someone trapped behind it. A grinder can cut through metal doors, while a sledgehammer is useful for breaking down walls.

 Fire hose
When the firefighters reach the fire, they unwind a long hose and plug it into a fire hydrant on the street for a supply of water (some trucks carry their own water source).

HOUSE BOAT

A HOUSEBOAT IS A LONG BARGE THAT FLOATS ON A RIVER. IT CONTAINS BEDS, A BATHROOM, AND A KITCHEN—A FLOATING HOME!

01 Speed

Houseboats are slow, with a speed of around 6 to 8 miles per hour. It can take an entire day to travel 60 miles (which would only take about an hour by car), so passengers better not be in a hurry! But the slow pace of life is why some people love houseboats.

02 Engine room

The boat's motor is found in the engine room. Whether powered by fuel or electricity, the engine is low, steady, and energy-efficient.

03 Maintenance

The boat needs regular upkeep to keep it in working condition: welding, mechanics, carpentry, plumbing, and painting. The work is essential and sometimes quite expensive.

04 Mooring ropes

These ropes, with a wide loop at each end, are used to tie the boat to the bank during a stopover and secure it to the lock so that it doesn't move. The ropes are at the front and the rear of the boat.

05 Ballast

Weights of 30 to 40 tons are placed between the boat's deck and its base to make it more stable and prevent it from pitching. This ballast also pushes the barge an additional 20 inches into the water, helping it fit underneath bridges without hitting them.

06 Boat-dwellers

People who live on houseboats have a different way of life, away from the rest of society. Boat-dwellers live alongside nature and love the water: its lapping movement is soothing, waves create the rhythm of their day, and its reflections illuminate their home. Often boats are moored together to form small "villages" with the community supporting one another.

07 Danger

Drifting tree trunks can damage the boat's hull, while fast-flowing water can pull down bridges or moorings. The barge may also run into the riverbed, so when floodwater recedes, the boats often find themselves stranded and stuck.

Shore power
The barge can be docked against a bank where terminals provide it with water and electricity. To be self-sufficient, a barge must have a generator, which uses fuel to produce electricity that is then stored in batteries. The flaw in this method is that the generator smokes and splutters.

Wheelhouse
The wheelhouse is the boat's cockpit. To steer the barge, one turns the ship's wheel made of wood or cast iron. The boat's size and weight make it slow to respond and difficult to direct, and without brakes, it can only be stopped by using the reverse gear. Strict rules also need to be followed: sail in the center of the waterway, overtake on the right, and slow down when near fisherman so as not to disturb the fish!

Bedroom
A barge can be very big, even as big as 1,800 square feet, or the size of a large house with a terrace—plenty of room for the whole family.

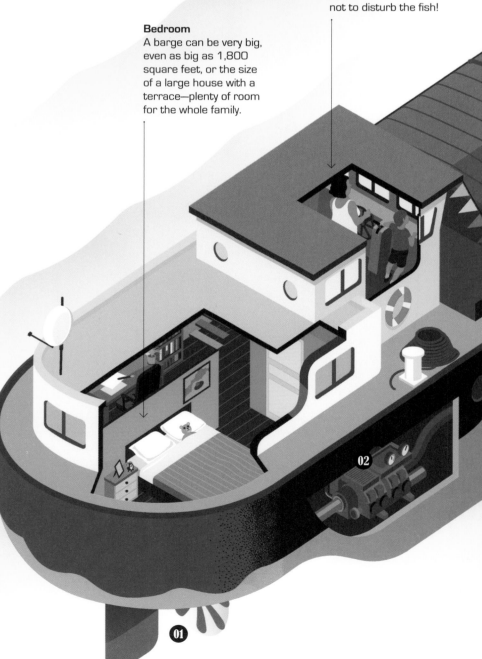

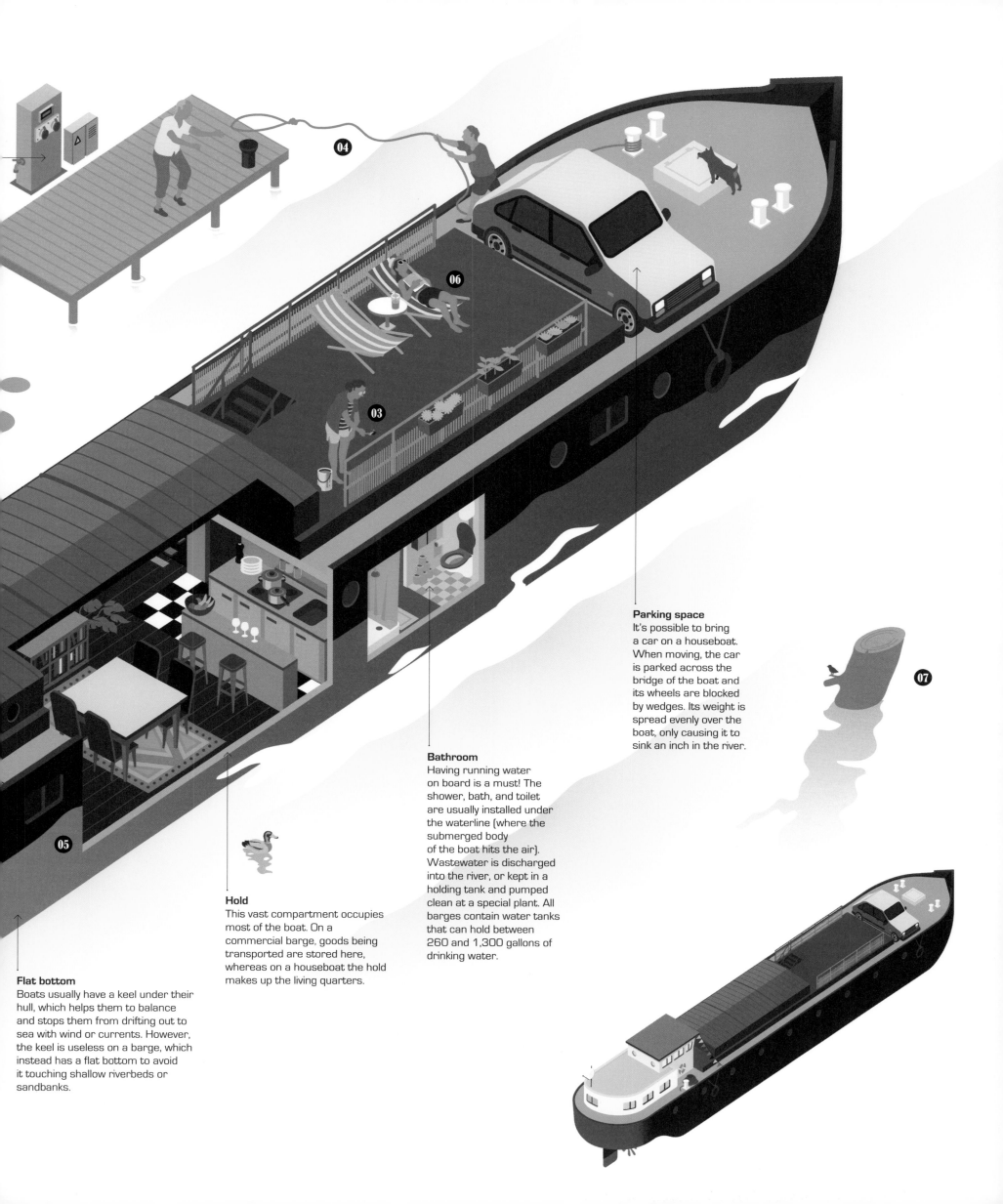

04

06

03

05

07

Parking space
It's possible to bring a car on a houseboat. When moving, the car is parked across the bridge of the boat and its wheels are blocked by wedges. Its weight is spread evenly over the boat, only causing it to sink an inch in the river.

Bathroom
Having running water on board is a must! The shower, bath, and toilet are usually installed under the waterline (where the submerged body of the boat hits the air). Wastewater is discharged into the river, or kept in a holding tank and pumped clean at a special plant. All barges contain water tanks that can hold between 260 and 1,300 gallons of drinking water.

Hold
This vast compartment occupies most of the boat. On a commercial barge, goods being transported are stored here, whereas on a houseboat the hold makes up the living quarters.

Flat bottom
Boats usually have a keel under their hull, which helps them to balance and stops them from drifting out to sea with wind or currents. However, the keel is useless on a barge, which instead has a flat bottom to avoid it touching shallow riverbeds or sandbanks.

AIRBUS A380

THE LONGEST, WIDEST, AND HEAVIEST AIRPLANE EVER TO BE MANUFACTURED IN THE WORLD. THIS CHAMPION IS MADE IN EUROPE.

01 Speed
Flying at approximately 620 miles per hour, this plane can travel nonstop from New York to Hong Kong—a distance of 8,000 miles.

02 Double-decker
The first of its kind, the A380 has two floors that passengers can board simultaneously. The main deck, on the bottom, connects to the upper deck by two flights of stairs at the front and rear of the cabin.

03 Flight instruments
Two sets of flight screens allow the pilot and copilot to work in tandem. They show the speed, altitude, and tilt of the plane, while the Flight Management System is the computer or "autopilot" that controls the plane according to the pilot's instructions.

04 Upper deck
The A380 is the only jet aircraft with an upper deck that runs the full length of the plane. This means the cabin has 50% more space when compared to the Boeing 747.

05 Fuselage
To lighten the plane, the alloy metal materials were replaced by composites (mixtures of materials, including plastic). A lightweight and shock-resistant fiberglass composite covers the fuselage.

Wings
The largest wings ever produced for a commercial airliner: their wingspan is 262 feet (the length of nine buses), and their surface area measures 9,100 square feet (equal to two basketball courts).

Jet engines
Four turbojets propel the plane into flight. Each of these engines has the power equivalent of around 1,500 cars even though their air intake is equal to that of the Airbus A320, the A380's little brother.

Pilots
In the cockpit, the pilot and copilot are in charge of the flight. Pilots need to be in excellent physical shape, have good nerves, and be cool-headed and composed in an emergency.

Landing gear
Weighing 600 tons when full (the same as about 100 elephants!), the A380's landing equipment is made up of 22 wheels that spread the enormous weight of the plane evenly as it touches down.

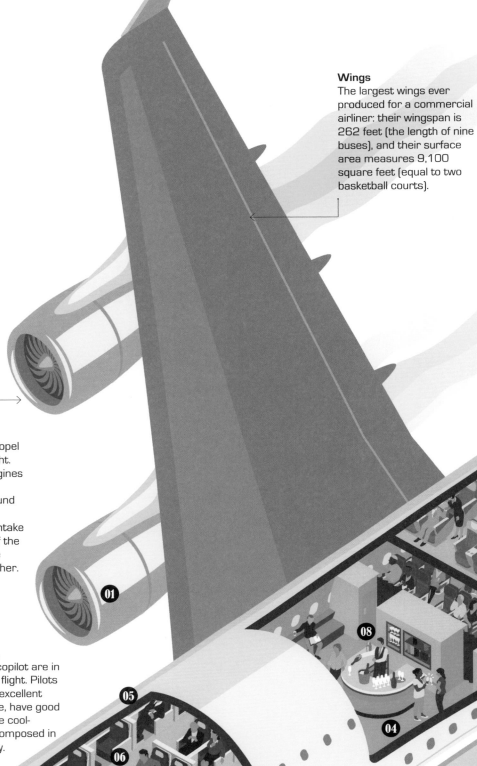

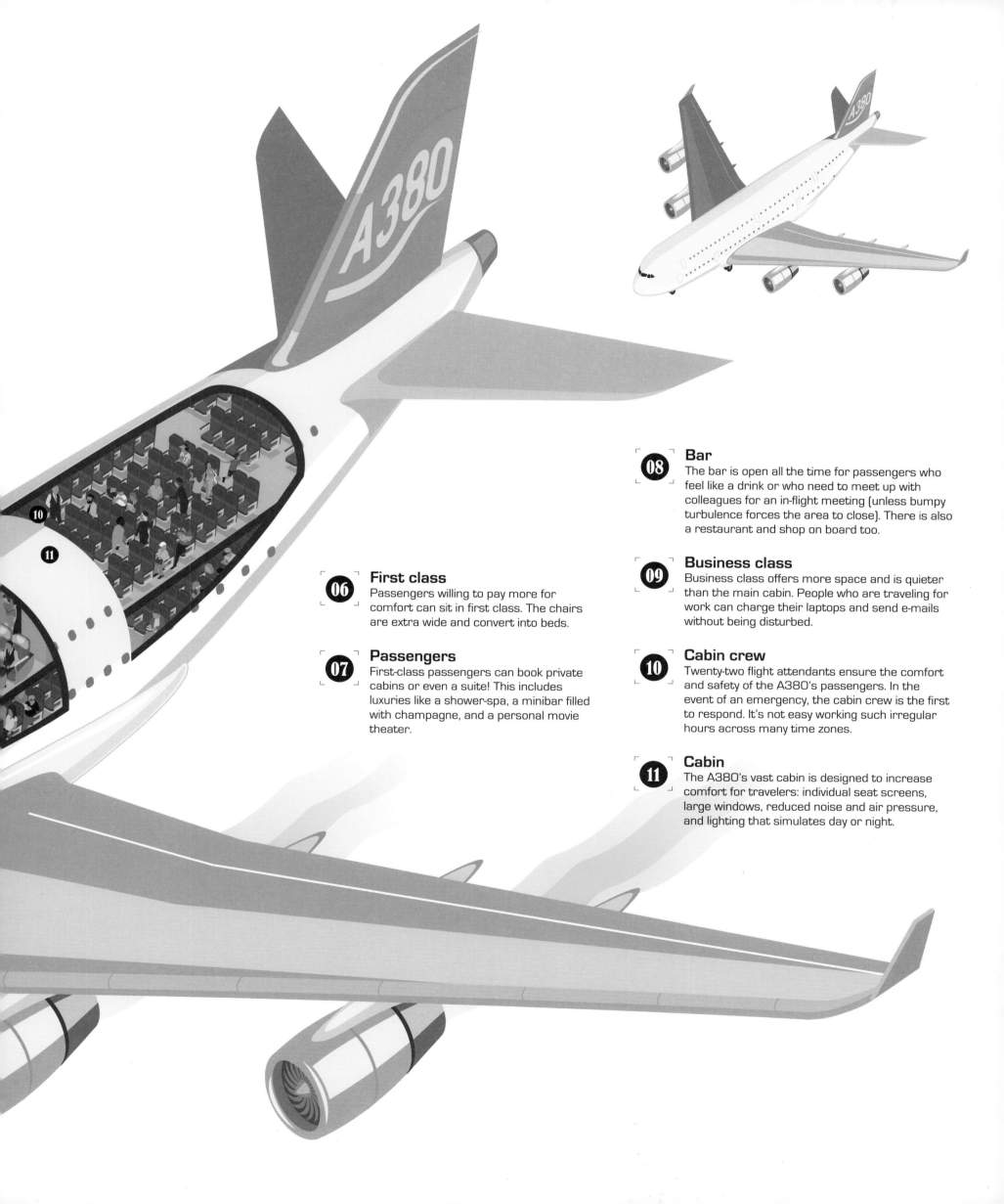

08 **Bar**
The bar is open all the time for passengers who feel like a drink or who need to meet up with colleagues for an in-flight meeting (unless bumpy turbulence forces the area to close). There is also a restaurant and shop on board too.

09 **Business class**
Business class offers more space and is quieter than the main cabin. People who are traveling for work can charge their laptops and send e-mails without being disturbed.

06 **First class**
Passengers willing to pay more for comfort can sit in first class. The chairs are extra wide and convert into beds.

07 **Passengers**
First-class passengers can book private cabins or even a suite! This includes luxuries like a shower-spa, a minibar filled with champagne, and a personal movie theater.

10 **Cabin crew**
Twenty-two flight attendants ensure the comfort and safety of the A380's passengers. In the event of an emergency, the cabin crew is the first to respond. It's not easy working such irregular hours across many time zones.

11 **Cabin**
The A380's vast cabin is designed to increase comfort for travelers: individual seat screens, large windows, reduced noise and air pressure, and lighting that simulates day or night.

CIRCUS
CONVOY

THE CIRCUS IS COMING TO TOWN! ARRIVING IN CONVOY, THESE CAGES, TENTS, AND HOUSES ON WHEELS TRANSPORT EVERYTHING: FROM EQUIPMENT TO ARTISTS, FROM ELEPHANTS TO POPCORN.

01 In convoy
Traveling circuses sometimes drive along roads in a chain as long as 2.5 miles! Their trucks are so wide that it is difficult for them to navigate narrow roads or to overtake other vehicles, which can lead to fender benders and collisions.

02 School
The children of performers travel wherever their parents go. The youngest ones go to school in a special mobile truck. Older children take online courses in the morning, before performing in the afternoons and evenings.

03 Box office
Before watching the circus, audience members buy their tickets at the box office. To set it up, the box office is lifted out of a truck using a hoist—a kind of mini crane. The cranes themselves are transported in a separate truck!

Big cats

An animal trainer has to earn the cats' trust and forge deep relationships with them. They need to be patient—it takes years to get results. They need to understand the animals' personality and always be alert to potential danger and accidents. When one tamer tried to kiss a lioness during a show, he accidently caught one of her fangs...A mistake that cost the trainer 13 stitches.

Menagerie

Classical circuses include dozens of animals, like elephants, llamas, horses, camels, tigers, and lions. All of these creatures travel separately from one another. It is the trainer's responsibility to care for these animals. Many animal welfare associations believe animal training is cruel and urge circuses to stop using wild animals in their shows.

On the road

Over the course of a year, a circus might tour for up to ten months. Every week they will visit around three new towns, and in the summer they might visit a new town every day.

Ringmaster

The ringmaster has a lot of responsibilities: they organize the tour, hire performers, sign contracts, manage the budget, and solve any problems that might come up. A ringmaster must have authority but also be sensitive to everyone's needs. A circus troupe is just like a big family!

The life of an artist

Every morning, the artists rehearse their acts under the big top—there is always room for improvement. The performers, who come from all over the world, give their very best to wow the audeince. For the show to be a success, everyone needs to enjoy working together!

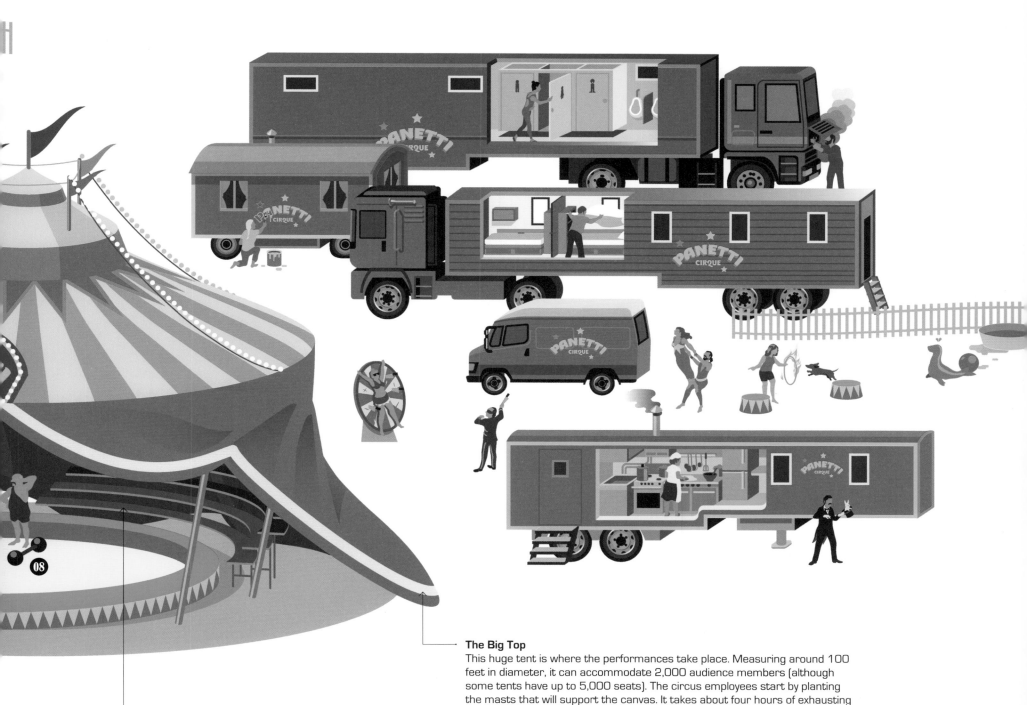

The Big Top
This huge tent is where the performances take place. Measuring around 100 feet in diameter, it can accommodate 2,000 audience members (although some tents have up to 5,000 seats). The circus employees start by planting the masts that will support the canvas. It takes about four hours of exhausting work to erect the tent and two hours to disassemble.

Tiered seating
These staggered benches are for the audience: they are mounted in a circle all around the circus tent. A meticulous task that leaves no room for error: the seating must not collapse under the weight of all the people! Sometimes private boxes are set up so some audience members can sit separately from the rest of the crowd.

TUNNEL BORING MACHINE

THIS COLOSSAL ENGINE IS USED TO EXCAVATE TUNNELS BY DIGGING FORWARD INTO ROCK AND PASSING BACK DEBRIS TO THE SURFACE.

01 Digging difficulties
It's not easy working deep below the ground: the heat is staggering, the noise is deafening, and dust constantly swirls around. There is very little space, and with no natural daylight, the only way to see is with bright neon lights.

02 A giant!
A tunnel boring machine (TBM) measures around 30 feet tall, 650 feet long (equal to ten semi-trailer trucks), and weighs approximately 1,000 tons (equal to 800 cars). Amazingly, there are even bigger boring machines than this! There are also some smaller ones that are used to dig narrower tunnels like those needed for sewage systems.

03 The speed of excavation
The TBM works slowly and steadily, advancing about 50 feet per day. If it manages 80 feet in one day, the whole team celebrates!

04 Pipe or clearing conveyor belt
Millions of cubic feet of mud and rock are extracted by the tunnel boring machine. This debris is mixed with water and pumped at high pressure along pipes and transported to the surface. Sometimes the rock is crushed and then evacuated by conveyor belt.

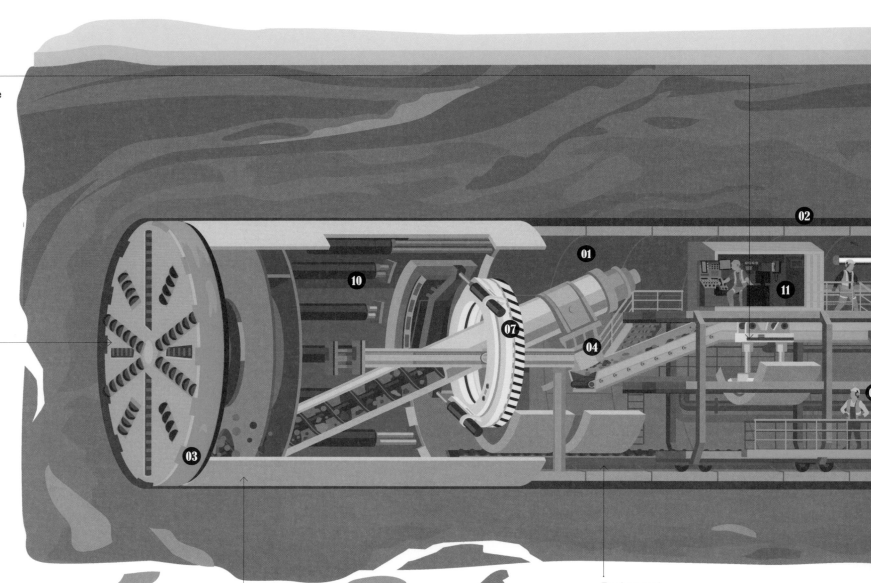

Crane and concrete segments
These reinforced concrete arches are 15 inches thick and will support the tunnel's walls and form its surface. The pieces are lifted into place by the TBM's crane as it progresses underground.

Cutting wheel
Turning on itself, this giant wheel drills all types of soils and rocks, using its 57 wheels and 150 sharp knives, spread over its head. It is equipped with several very powerful electric motors.

Shield
The shield is a watertight and ultra-resistant partition that encases the mechanisms enabling the TBM to excavate. It turns the cutting wheel and extracts the debris.

Backup train
The backup train moves along rails inside the TBM. It is used as transportation to and from the cockpit, as well as moving the support arches and the hydraulic and electrical materials and carrying the mortar tanks, oil, and ventilation systems from the tunnel surface.

The team
Electricians, engineers, mechanics, topographers, and machine operators all work together to dig the tunnel. Team spirit is essential for the smooth running of the project. The TBMs are also sometimes given nicknames like "Bertha" or "Helene," for good luck!

A delicate job
The digging of a tunnel must be structurally perfect and comply with strict safety rules: there can be no risk of the tunnel collapsing! In order to dig, the team must adapt to the terrain, whether hard or soft, sandy or muddy, while making sure not to disrupt the tunnel's surrounding environment.

Erector
Like a giant suction cup, the erector positions the concrete arches that will form the tunnel.

Ventilation duct
In such a tight space, pure air runs out quickly. To combat this problem, the ventilation duct pumps the site with a constant flow of clean air from outside the tunnel. It is also necessary to remove concrete dust, dirt, diesel fumes from mobile machinery, and various dangerous gases from the air. If everything works smoothly, there should be no need for protective masks.

Hidden treasure
At the start of a tunnel project, archaeological digs are often organized. When the Channel Tunnel was being dug, archaeologists discovered tombs and weapons dating from the Middle Ages. Workers have also discovered fossils as old as 95 million years!

Thrust cylinder
A hydraulic thrust cylinder contains a moving piston rod that can push or pull loads. Here, the cylinders are used to brace against the gripper and push the machine forward. The cylinders create a pushing force of around 6,000 tons!

Cockpit
Surrounded by screens and computers, the pilot directs the TBM with the utmost precision. The pilot is also the link between all the team members, passing information between those underground and on the surface. They are also responsible for ensuring no mistakes take place.

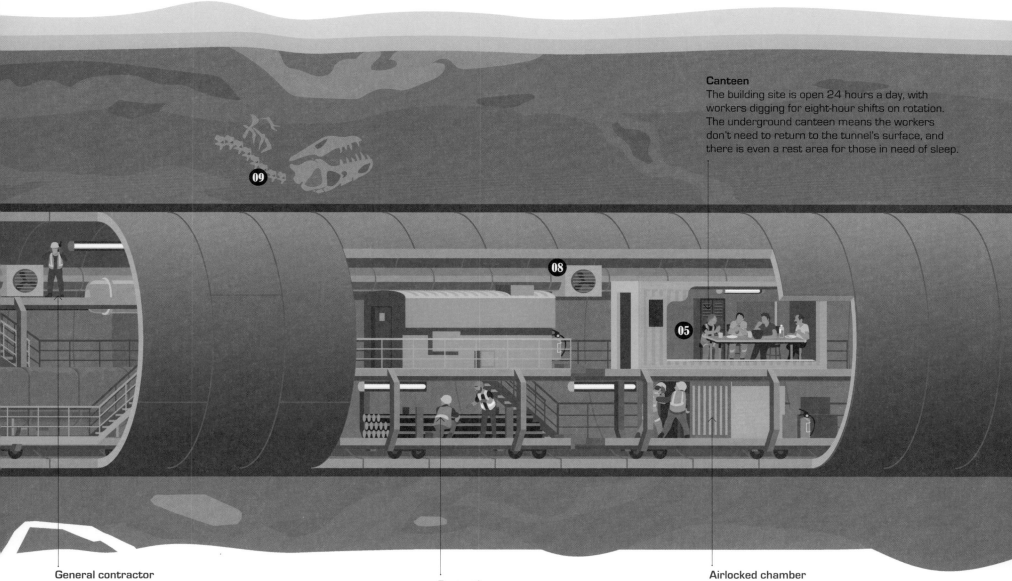

Canteen
The building site is open 24 hours a day, with workers digging for eight-hour shifts on rotation. The underground canteen means the workers don't need to return to the tunnel's surface, and there is even a rest area for those in need of sleep.

General contractor
A general contractor is the person (or company) responsible for carrying out the work. They design the plans, decide the technical strategy, and delegate the work. In short, they manage everything, including the deadline and making sure the project stays on budget. Digging a tunnel costs a fortune!

Protective gear
To ensure their protection, workers wear fireproof overalls, safety shoes, earplugs, and anti-shock helmets with visors to protect their eyes.

Airlocked chamber
One of the biggest fears of the tunnel diggers is that a fire might break out. If this were to happen, the workers can quickly escape the flames and smoke in the airlocked chamber. Totally airtight, with its own electricity source, water, and oxygen, it can accommodate 20 people for several hours.

GLOSSARY

Accommodate
To provide enough space for something.

Aerodynamic
The study of the properties of moving air and the interaction between the air and solid things moving through it.

Ammunition
A supply of bullets or shells.

Anchorage
An area off the coast that is suitable for a ship to anchor or the act of securing something to a base.

Antenna
A rod, wire, or other structure through which signals are transmitted or received, usually as part of a radio transmission or receiving system.

Armament
Military weapons and equipment.

Archaeologist
Someone who studies history through the excavation of sites and the study of artifacts and other physical remains.

Art nouveau
A style of decorative art and architecture popular from about 1890 until World War I.

Ascend
To go up or to climb.

Astrolabe
An instrument used to make astronomical measurements, usually about the position of planets and stars in the night sky.

Astronomy
A science that studies celestial objects, space, and the universe in great detail.

Autonomous
Acting independently.

Auxiliary
Something that provides additional help and support.

Ballast
Heavy material placed near a ship's hull to make sure it is stable.

Bandit
A robber belonging to a gang that breaks the law.

Caliber
The internal diameter of a gun barrel.

Capsize
When a boat overturns in the water so it is completely upside down.

Capsule
A small case or container that is usually round in shape.

Carbon monoxide
A colorless, odorless toxic flammable gas formed by incomplete combustion of carbon.

Cargo
Goods carried on a ship, aircraft, or any other type of motor vehicle.

Charcoal
A black carbon material obtained by heating wood or other organic matter.

Claustrophobic
Someone who is extremely afraid of small, confined spaces.

Colossal
Extremely large.

Cyclone
A very strong, rotating windstorm.

Debris
Scattered pieces of trash.

Descend
To go down.

Dimension
A specific kind of measurement, such as length, breadth, depth, or height.

Emulsifier
Something that helps form an emulsion (a mixture of two liquids that would not normally mix).

Enamel
A smooth glossy coating that resembles a ceramic glaze.

En route
On the way.

En-suite
When a bathroom and bedroom are connected, forming part of the same set of rooms.

Epitome
A person or thing that is a perfect example of a quality.

Excavate
To remove earth carefully from an area.

Evacuate
To remove people from a place of danger and go to a safer place.

Evaporate
When liquid turns into vapor.

Flammable
Something that is easily set on fire.

Fuselage
The main body of an aircraft.

Galley
A low, flat ship with one or more sails, often used for war or piracy.

Girders
A large iron or steel beam structure, often used for building bridges and the framework of large buildings.

Helmsman
Someone who steers a ship or boat.

Hydrant
A small structure in a street or other public place with a nozzle that a hose can attach to in order to access the water mains.

Hydrogen
A colorless, odorless, highly flammable gas.

Iceberg
A large floating lump of ice.

Ignite
To catch fire or cause something to catch fire.

Immigrant
A person from a different country who comes to live permanently in a foreign country.

Keel
The lengthwise timber or steel structure along the base of a ship, supporting the framework of the whole ship.

Kerosene
A type of fuel used especially in jet engines and domestic heating boilers.

Lacquer
A type of liquid that dries to form a hard, protective coating for wood, metal, and other surfaces.

Launcher
A structure that holds a rocket or missile.

Locomotive
A powered railway vehicle used for pulling trains.